THIS BOOK BELONGS TO:

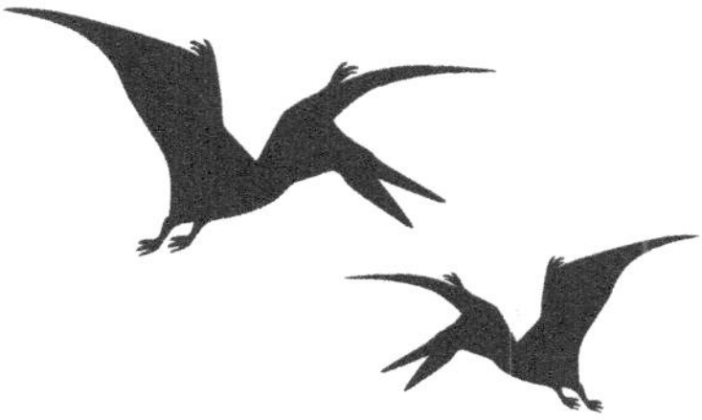

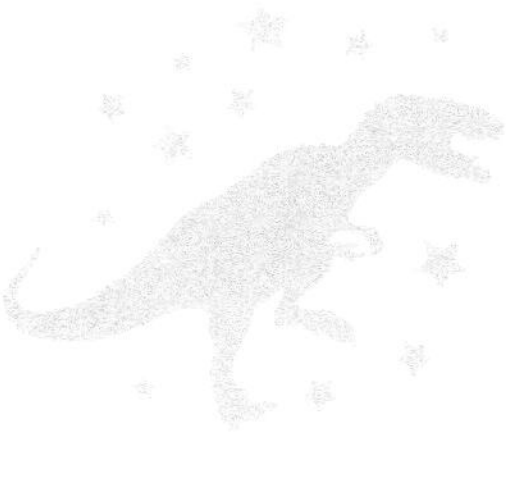

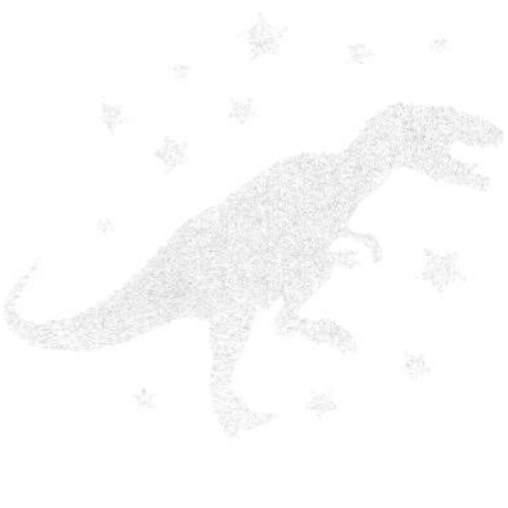

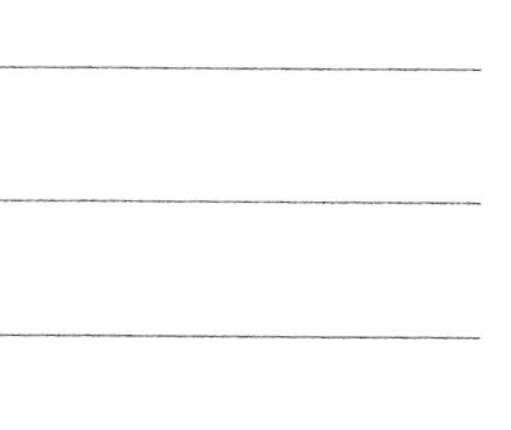

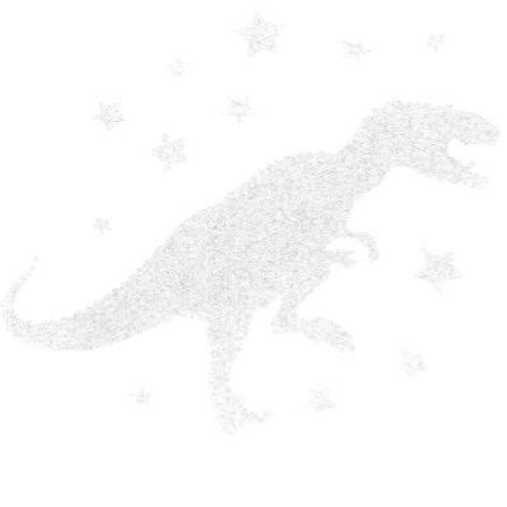

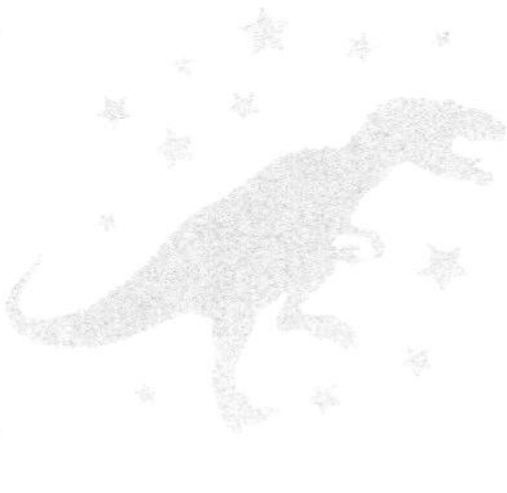

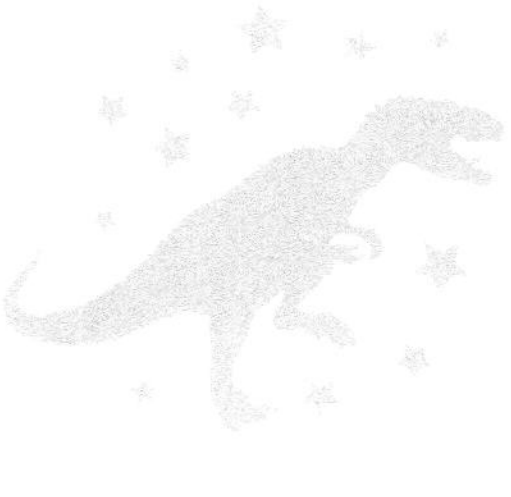

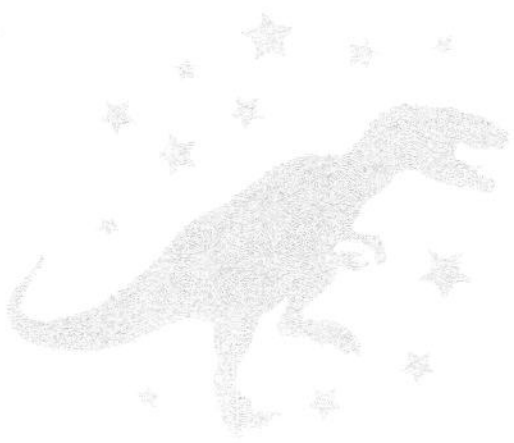

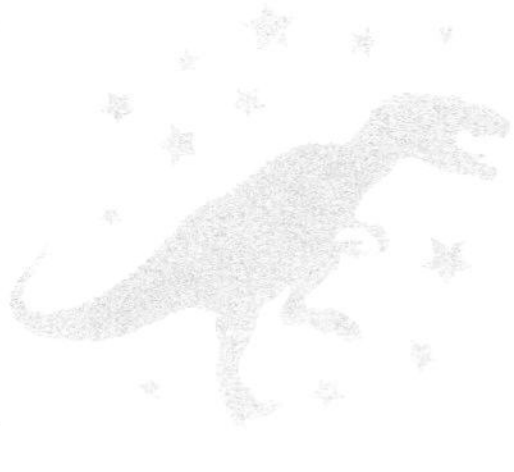

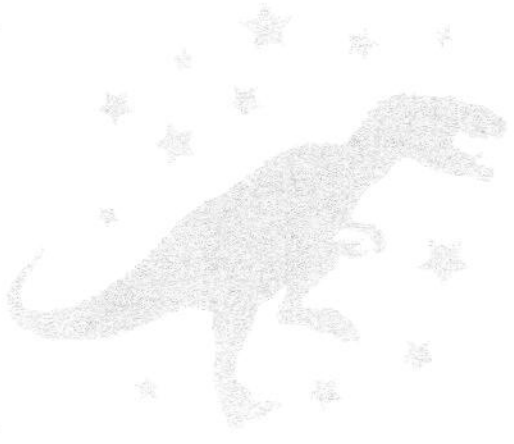

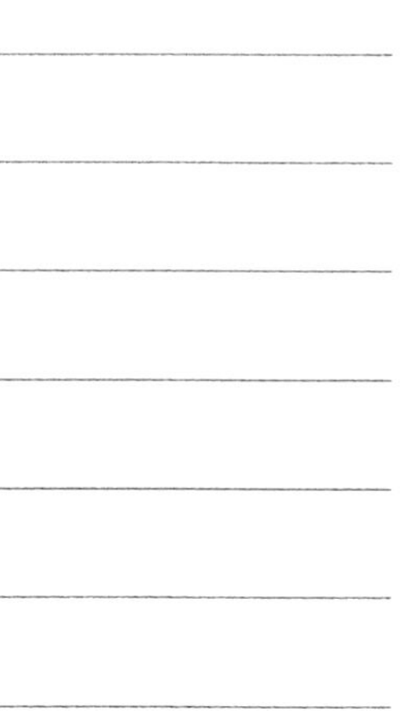

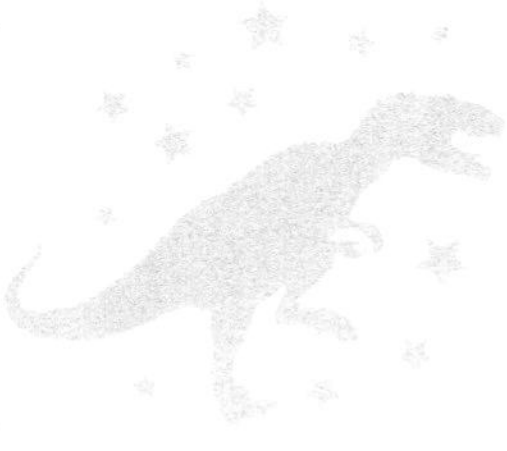

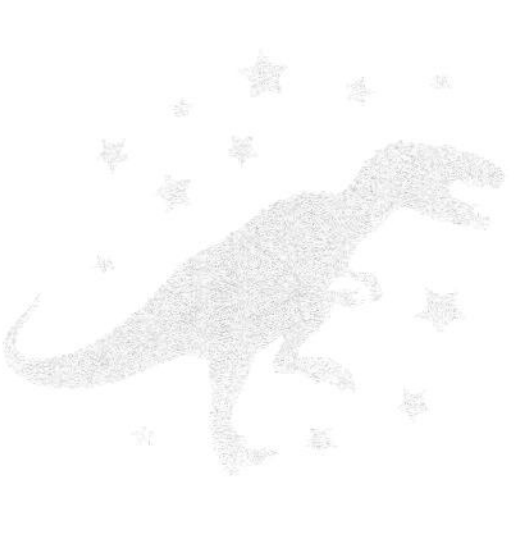

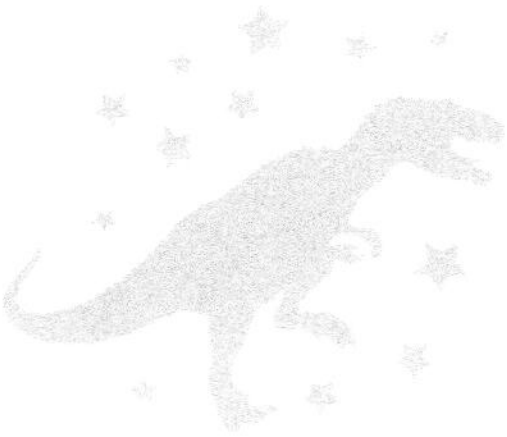

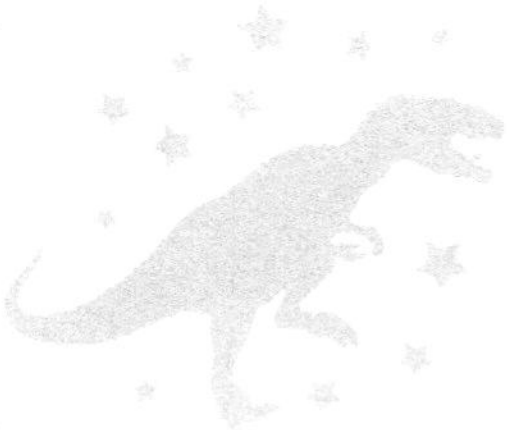

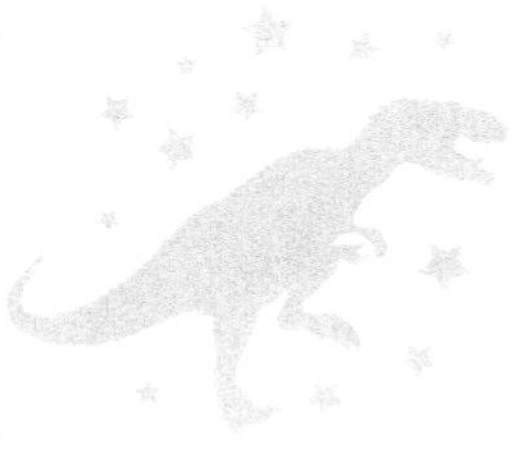

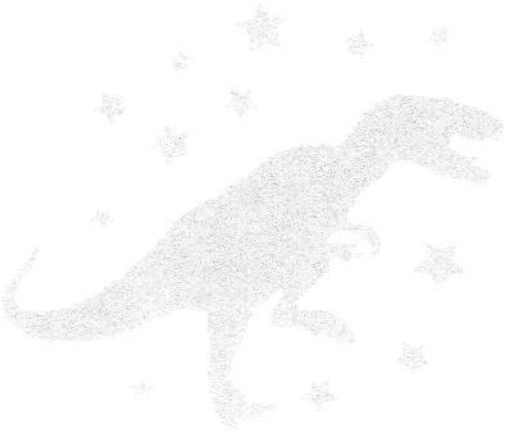

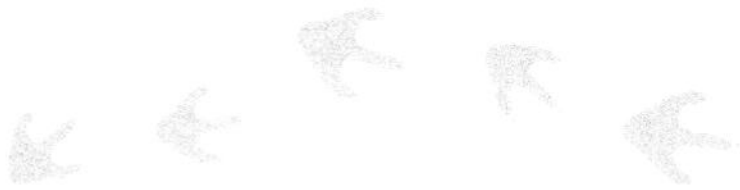

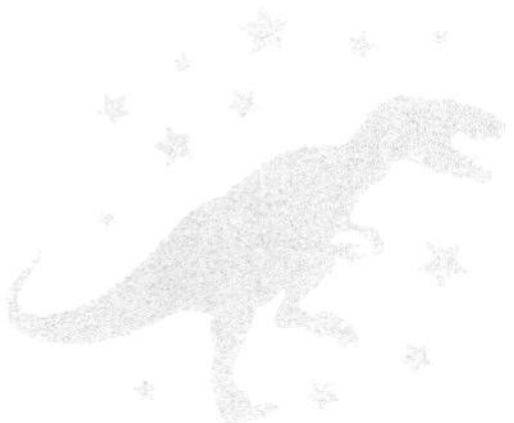

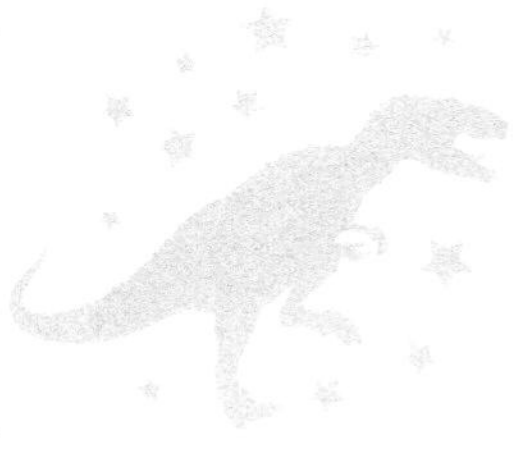

Made in the USA
Las Vegas, NV
27 May 2024

90453887R00069